25 Christmas Songs for Marimba

ISBN 978-1-5400-9765-1

Visit Hal Leonard Online at
www.halleonard.com

Contact us:
Hal Leonard
7777 West Bluemound Road
Milwaukee, WI 53213
Email: info@halleonard.com

In Europe, contact:
Hal Leonard Europe Limited
42 Wigmore Street
Marylebone, London, W1U 2RN
Email: info@halleonardeurope.com

In Australia, contact:
Hal Leonard Australia Pty. Ltd.
4 Lentara Court
Cheltenham, Victoria, 3192 Australia
Email: info@halleonard.com.au

ALL I WANT FOR CHRISTMAS IS YOU

MARIMBA

Words and Music by MARIAH CAREY
and WALTER AFANASIEFF

BLUE CHRISTMAS

Marimba

Words and Music by BILLY HAYES
and JAY JOHNSON

HAVE YOURSELF A MERRY LITTLE CHRISTMAS

from MEET ME IN ST. LOUIS

Marimba

Words and Music by HUGH MARTIN
and RALPH BLANE

CHRISTMAS IN KILLARNEY

MARIMBA

Words and Music by JOHN REDMOND
and FRANK WELDON

THE CHRISTMAS SONG
(Chestnuts Roasting on an Open Fire)

Marimba

Music and Lyric by MEL TORMÉ
and ROBERT WELLS

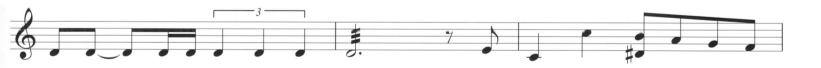

FELIZ NAVIDAD

MARIMBA

Music and Lyrics by
JOSÉ FELICIANO

FROSTY THE SNOW MAN

MARIMBA

Words and Music by STEVE NELSON
and JACK ROLLINS

HERE COMES SANTA CLAUS
(Right Down Santa Claus Lane)

MARIMBA

Words and Music by GENE AUTRY
and OAKLEY HALDEMAN

I HEARD THE BELLS ON CHRISTMAS DAY

Marimba

Words by HENRY WADSWORTH LONGFELLOW
Adapted by JOHNNY MARKS
Music by JOHNNY MARKS

I SAW MOMMY KISSING SANTA CLAUS

MARIMBA

Words and Music by
TOMMIE CONNOR

I WONDER AS I WANDER

MARIMBA

By JOHN JACOB NILES

I'LL BE HOME FOR CHRISTMAS

MARIMBA

Words and Music by KIM GANNON
and WALTER KENT

IT'S BEGINNING TO LOOK LIKE CHRISTMAS

MARIMBA

Words and Music by
MEREDITH WILLSON

JINGLE BELL ROCK

MARIMBA

Words and Music by JOE BEAL
and JIM BOOTHE

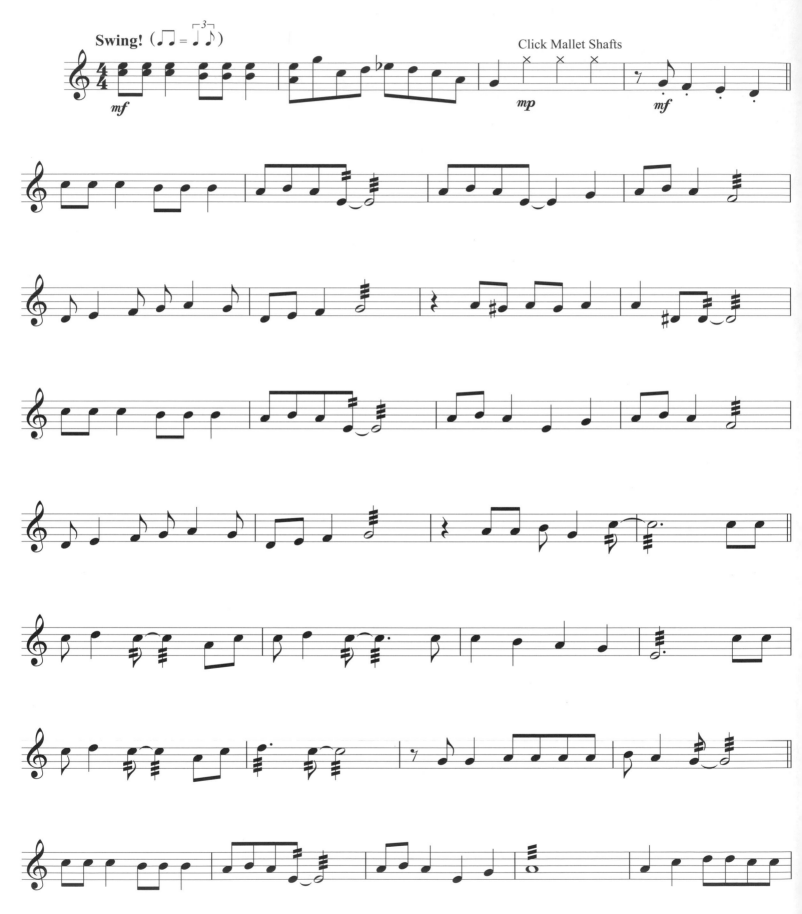

Click Mallet Shafts

LET IT SNOW! LET IT SNOW! LET IT SNOW!

MARIMBA

Words by SAMMY CAHN
Music by JULE STYNE

THE LITTLE DRUMMER BOY

Marimba

Words and Music by HARRY SIMEONE,
HENRY ONORATI and KATHERINE DAVIS

MELE KALIKIMAKA

MARIMBA

Words and Music by
R. ALEX ANDERSON

ROCKIN' AROUND THE CHRISTMAS TREE

MARIMBA

Music and Lyrics by
JOHNNY MARKS

RUDOLPH THE RED-NOSED REINDEER

MARIMBA

Music and Lyrics by
JOHNNY MARKS

SANTA CLAUS IS COMIN' TO TOWN

Marimba

Words by HAVEN GILLESPIE
Music by J. FRED COOTS

SANTA BABY

MARIMBA

By JOAN JAVITS,
PHIL SPRINGER and TONY SPRINGER

(Opt. double stops)

(Opt. double stops)

SLEIGH RIDE

Marimba

Music by LEROY ANDERSON
Words by MITCHELL PARISH

WHITE CHRISTMAS
from the Motion Picture Irving Berlin's HOLIDAY INN

MARIMBA

Words and Music by
IRVING BERLIN

Moderately slow, in 2

WE NEED A LITTLE CHRISTMAS
from MAME

Marimba

Music and Lyric by
JERRY HERMAN

Lively, with a two-beat feel

YOU'RE A MEAN ONE, MR. GRINCH

from DR. SEUSS' HOW THE GRINCH STOLE CHRISTMAS

Marimba

Lyrics by DR. SEUSS
Music by ALBERT HAGUE